Slapstick
Gravitas

Slapstick Gravitas

Selected Spells, Centos, Lists and Other Poems

Mikhail Horowitz

Station Hill Press
BARRYTOWN, NY

Published by Station Hill Press, the publishing project of the Institute for Publishing Arts, Inc., 120 Station Hill Road, Barrytown, NY 12507, New York, a not-for-profit, tax-exempt organization [501(c)(3)].

Online catalogue: www.stationhill.org
e-mail: publishers@stationhill.org

Cover collage by Mikhail Horowitz
Cover and interior design by Susan Quasha

Author Photo: Jennifer May

Some of these poems and texts appeared in the following print and/or online publications: Abraxas, Blazing Stadium, The Cento, The Doris, Hunger, In|filtration: An Anthology of Innovative Poetry from the Hudson River Valley, Jewish Currents, Long Shot, Matter, Metambesen, Open Space, Track Life, and Ulster Magazine.

The author is deeply indebted to the Station Hill team—George and Susan Quasha and Sam Truitt—for bringing this book to life.

Library of Congress Cataloging-in-Publication Data

Names: Horowitz, Mikhail, author.
Title: Slapstick gravitas : selected spells, centos, and lists / Mikhail Horowitz.
Identifiers: LCCN 2021032906 | ISBN 9781581772104 (paperback)
Subjects: LCGFT: Poetry. | Creative nonfiction.
Classification: LCC PS3558.O6943 S57 2021 | DDC 811/.54—dc23
LC record available at https://lccn.loc.gov/2021032906

Contents

Preface

The great Chilean poet Nicanor Parra wrote, *En poesia se permite todo* ("In poetry everything is permitted"), which I take as a seal of approval, as if any were needed, to engage in experimental writing and/or the wholesale pillaging of poetic forms. Simply stated, my m.o. has always been to take whatever I can, wherever and whenever I can, from whomever I can—but always to give credit. Hence, over the course of more than five decades of writing poetry, I have cross-pollinated (or lowered property values) in many meadows, invoking or embodying an English Romantic poet of the early 19th century, a Chinese hermit poet of the Tang Dynasty, a neo-Beat jazz poet of the Third Millennium, a Surrealist or Oulipo poet of Paris between the wars, and a postmodern poet and spoken-word performer in an increasingly tone-deaf America.

The works here represent a wide selection of writings by my various avatars, spanning a period from my juvenilia of the early 1970s to my juvenilia of last week. They embrace a plethora of forms and approaches, ranging from formal sonnets to projective verse to appropriations from my betters to pieces written specifically for performance. Writing, reading, and reciting poetry has been my raison d'être, my daily practice, my indissoluble bond to a multilingual, pangalactic community of kindred spirits, my escape from encroaching decrepitude as well as my embrace of it, my way to make love to the world, my continuing source of messy revelation, my "momentary taste of Being from the well amid the waste," and the terms of my service to the present time-track. Recently, during the height of the pandemic, I was asked if I was an essential worker. I replied, I'm a poet—what do *you* think?

Slapstick
Gravitas

I. Spells

For Gilles Malkine, Oulipoet malgre lui

Art

Always ready to
arrive, reclaiming territory
and risking total
annihilation, rejecting those
antiquated representations, then
accepting representational tendencies
anew, renovating these
abstract rooms, tracing
a red thought
along rivers that
are radically translated,
altering roses, thickening
apples, rendering time
as rumpled turquoise,
abrading radiance through
all Raphael's trembling
angels right to
Archipenko, Rodchenko, Tatlin,
also rediscovering Turner's
atmospherics. Reality teases
artists, ridicules their
aspirations, resists talent,
abnegates responsibility. Then
again, Rauschenberg transfers
Arcimboldo's Renaissance tomatoes
and rutabagas to
assemblages; Rembrandt tells
Andy, Really, try
affecting richer textures—
art relishes truth
and rewards trickery,
a rare thing.

Myth

Make yourself timeless. How
Moon yellows the hills,
Makes your torn hands
Meander, your tongue hairy.
Might you torture her.
Might you transform her,
Meaning yew. The hell
Mouth yawns, then howls
Music—yours. The horned
Mare yanks the halter,
Makes *you* the hunted,
Marks your trembling. Her
Mother yelps; the hag
Means you terrible harm.
Might you tickle her.
Might your trickery have
Many yellow teeth. How
Moon yokes those heavenly
Monsters, your tiger horses.
Mask your treachery, holy
Man. Your torn heart.
Make yourself the hero.

Words

Writers overestimate readers? Don't say.
Without old rhythms, dem syllables,
Written on reeds, don't scan.
We only revive dead sentences.
Wholly original? Really, dear—such
Wapdoodle offends Rimbaud, Dickinson, Sartre,
Whitman, Oates, Robert Duncan, Szymborska,
Wonderful others reifying death, simultaneously
Wakening our repressed desires ... so
Write of rich, dark, sensuous
Worlds, oddly, richly, darkly, sensuously

Dreams

Descend, remembering Eurydice, alabaster mountains, scrambling
Down rocky escarpments and murky streets,
Deeper, rapid eye (atemporal) movement, summoning
Darker regions, eidolons, apparitions, metempsychotic states:
Dangerous roads end abruptly. Maybe. Seven
Dead relatives enter as many sunken
Doorways, revenants expressing all my stifled
Desires, recalling every animal mankind still
Detests. Reptile eats another mother. Seven
Dead reptiles enter as many shrunken
Dicks, reclaiming each as mine. Sperm
Dries, rooms empty. A moth—Sphinx—
Does reels, embraces Aunt Matilda, sadly.
Drapes rustle. Emily arrives, menacing seven
Dead ... rutabagas? Everything almost means something,
Doesn't remain, escapes ... ah Morpheus, subterranean
Deceiver, reticent entity, approach me, slowly,
Dawn reddens embryonic avenues, muted senses
Drift; restore Endymion's antique mind, sleep ...
Don't really ever awake me, slipping ...

Beckett

Begin end: candles kindly extinguished. Time to
Bury everything, Clov. Kiss even this threadbare
Body—eroded, cold, knackered, enduring—ta-ta.
Because Estragon can't kill Estragon, the tree,
Barren, exits. Clowns know emptiness takes time.
Bones, embers, cinders … Krapp's echo: tinny. Tomorrow's
Bleak endgame compares keenly, exactly, to today's.

Adam & Eve

Another day, another morning & evening visits Eden.
Algae, daffodils, asters, mastodons & elephants, vireos, ernes,
Antelope, dragonflies, amanita mushrooms, & even various eels,
All deserving appellations. Mysterious & elegant, Viper enters:
Apple, dear? Apple's munched & eaten. Viper exits;
Almighty Deity appears: Man & Eve, vacate! Eftsoons,
A daunting archangel materializes & evicts vulnerable Eve
And deteriorating Adam. Me & everyone voyage elsewhere.

Last Words

Leaving all save the world. Oh ragged, disembodied soul,
Linger a space, to wing over rooftops, dropping silently,
Lightly, along some timelessly winding oblivion river. Don't
  struggle—
Lives are snowy tomes written on rice, dissolving, sans
Luminous angels, sans transcendence, without ongoing reveries,
  dreams, sweet
Longings, afterlife ... surrender this wildness of remembering,
  deliquesce, sip
Lethe and sense that well-oiled reality departing, splitting,
Leaving all save these words. Oh remnant, deflecting silence.

Mother Nature

Musician of Terra's heart; elderly registered nurse attending to un-
conscious, rejected elementals;

Magical Ops tending herds; eternal Rhiannon nimble and terrible,
uttering rocks, efts,

Mountains, owls, trees; Hathor embodied, richly nurturing all
things, unendingly relishing Eros;

Mad, ornery, tenacious hag eating rags, nightmarishly aspiring to
upend real estate—

Make of this human error residing nowhere a truthful, utterly real,
essentially

Meaningful offering to holy Earth, responsive now always to undy-
ing redemptive energies.

Blotter Entries

Black lumberjack, off the trail, entered racist enclave near Trois Rivieres, indiscriminately eviscerated seven

Blind lady on telephone, Tuesday evening, reported encountering nasty twosome rummaging in embroidery storeroom

Bespectacled local optometrist, Thursday, tennish, evidently robbed eleven neighbors, then ran into Eagle Scout

Biplane landed on Trenton Terrace, ensuing ruckus engaged nearly thirty responders, injuring (estimated) seventeen

Bobby Lee, of Twin Towers, enabled rogue elephant, Nabob, to rampage in East Sussex

Behind library, Officer Thompson tallied eight runaways emptying nine trashcans, releasing industrial effluvia (Sunday)

Belligerent, loaded, obese Trentonian threatened emaciated Rahway escapees numerous times, remarking, "I eradicate scumbags!"

II.   Homages

Borges

Old Spaniard speaking to an older Greek,
"Somos el tiempo," you say, and he
Steps once, twice into the mutable creek
Whose headlong rush bears everything away—
"Todo se aleja," you nod and laugh,
As gods and philosophers, thrones and souls,
Are swept with all else in the river's path,
As memory dims and the darkness falls—
"Somos el agua, somos el rio,"
Written in water, we do not endure;
Shakespeare, and Blake, and old Heraclito
Are foam on the waves and grains on the shore—
As blind, in one of your myriad selves,
You flow, in dreams, among endless bookshelves.

Cornell Box

The space enclosed by a Cornell box is the space enclosed by the letter o in the word *memory*. It is audible as well as visual space: one hears it in the half-sleep of remembering, the whispered confidings of a lost amour, floating back to ear's periwinkle at the strangest hours. There is no time in a Cornell box, any more than there is time in the imprint of a trilobite in limestone, or the image of sere leaves settling on discarded newspapers at the foot of an empty bandshell in the park. *Il est toujours six heures maintenant.* There is nothing to sweep up in a Cornell box, no work to be done, no skeletons to dress or hide. There is only the space enclosed by the letter o in the words *echo, poetry, ghost.*

René Magritte: Rap Sheet

This criminal mastermind, this Moriarty of paint, has picked logic's pocket, lifting its fat wallet of conventional thought and upsetting, in the process, the apple cart of cause and effect. Bad enough to con us into thinking that a pipe is not a pipe, that massive boulders in the Pyrenees can defy the laws of gravity, or that a man facing a mirror can see himself reflected from the back—but the true audacity of this miscreant lies in the hiding of his crimes *in plain sight*, on canvases that yield no fingerprints, no traces of DNA, nor any other mark that might convict him. In fact, he was arrested only once, on suspicion of stealing the key to dreams; but when they posed him for the mug shot, a white bird swooped in front of his face *just* as the shutter clicked.

from Lives of the Great Surrealists

I.

One day André Breton sought the services of a renowned soothsayer who lived in a garret on the Boulevard Bonne-Nouvelle. Having scried her crystal sphere, she announced that he had no future. Breton paid the sibyl her 500 francs and, repairing to the Café Fata Morgana, commissioned a young but already dissipated American poet, Hart Crane, to commit suicide in his place.

II.

Max Ernst and René Magritte were playing Scrabble. After contemplating the board, Ernst confidently placed a "W" above the "O" in ONEIRIC, adding an "R" and a "D" below the "O". "That is not a word," said Magritte.

III.

Duchamp's opponent sat down, and looked up: depending from the ceiling, directly above the empty chessboard, was a strip of flypaper, within whose sticky confines the 32 chessmen were caught. "I concede," he said.

IV.

A light bulb blew in the studio of Georges Malkine. Armed with a new bulb, the painter mounted a ladder. Just then Robert Desnos walked in and, assessing the situation, asked his friend, "Alors, how many Surrealist painters does it take to change a light bulb?" Malkine thought for a few seconds, and then muttered, "Votre mere, avec un poisson."*

---

*"Your mother, with a fish."

V.

It was a snowy morning in Bruxelles. The doughy snowman that Magritte had been building was almost complete. All it lacked was the black bowler hat that dignified the head of its creator. Magritte gave his bowler to the snowman and walked home. Throughout the night, and all the next day, and into the spring, and even during the long hot months of a particularly sultry summer, the snowman stood intact. Meanwhile, from the shoulders up, Magritte began to melt.

The Three Gone Conclusions

for Richard, Lord Buckley

Who drops us onto and into this sweetly swingin' sphere, enables us to chill here blowin' hot and cold, young and old, twice and thrice and ten times told for a designated number of spins around the sun, and then returns us, gradually or suddenly, to the mud and dust and grit and grain from whence we came?

Good question!

It is not Zeus, or Apollo, or the mighty Aphrodite, nor even, gents and ladies, the implacable cat who rules the eponymous Hades—but a trippin' trio of hip sisters that the ancient Attican hepcats called The Moirai, or, in plain English, the Fates, aka the Three Gone Conclusions. It is *these* three swingin' or should I say spinnin' sisters who make it, shake it, and break it for every homo- and hetero-sapiens beboppin' and freehoppin' through this amazingly lucid and irreducible journey that we call *life on Earth*.

Can you dig it?

Now the three principals of this mythical sisterhood work together as a team—each great lady has her own specialty, which only clicks when it is cookin' with the speciality of her two sisters. In other words, each of the three has a no-show ego but is rock-solid in the all-for-one-and-one-for-all department—no stars, no divas, no directors, but a very hip trinity of equal partners, diggin' their gig from here to infinity.

It all kicks off with Madame Clotho, the hip spinner who spins the tenuous thread of existence from her diaphanous distaff onto her splendid spindle. The distaff, you dig, contains the unspun fibers of life, and keeps them from getting jumbled, stuck, and otherwise hung up in the process of spinning.

Next up is Lady Lachesis, who cops a bit of thread from the spindle of her spinning sibling and stretches it out as far as it can boogie—two years, twenty years, a hundred years—and checks it against her measuring rod. Whatever the rod say, wherever that thread dead-ends and stops on a dime, that is the allotted time of the measuree, whether he or she be high and mighty or puny and impecunious, don't matter to Lady Lachesis, she cannot extend that thread another angstrom, baby!

Which leaves it all up to the tender mercy of Madame Atropos, who has, undeservedly, the baddest rap among the Three Gone Conclusions, because she is the breath-of-death thread-snipper, the scissor-handed-all-plans-ender, of every *life on Earth.* But dig it—who in the tight and righteous confines of their right minds would want that thread to be endless? To just keep growin' older and feebler, arthritic and paralytic, hip replacement, lip replacement, knee replacement, face replacement, trembling dementia, *'scuse me Junior, I'm immortal and in the way*— no way, we say! Let me die at my time allotted by the Three Gone Conclusions, as gracefully as possible under the willy-nilly, herky-jerky circumstances. So carpe diem, sweaty dudes and sweet dudettes—seize the day, because the gig ain't over until the fat Fate sings, or snips the strings.

To C.S., in Celebration

Earth, receive an honored guest—
Carolee is laid to rest,
Giving back her tigress heart
That would not compromise her art;
Back to dust her dancing skin
That let so many lovers in
And served as canvas, camera, clay,
For all the truths she dared to say,
And all the joys she laughed to seize
While pushing at the boundaries
With fierce compassion, gentle rage—
The bravest Artist of her Age.

Listening to Lindsay

ERICA LINDSAY QUINTET, ROSENDALE CAFÉ,
EARLY 1990S

she's
nefertiti
with a tenor
all chiseled
nobility
& egyptian
discipline

her fervor
burnishing
the orange nimbus
that warms the bell
of her horn

cooking
vigorous riffs
in canopic bistros
smoking
dusky clubs
with solar glyphs

right hand
feathering the valves
left hand
a sudden flutter
of bopped ostriches
& swung butterflies

both hands
smoldering
in a double lotus
of incorruptible
blowing

sculpting
a discursive serpent
at the ebony heart
of every inlaid
phrase

now crook
now flail
her saxophone flows
through niles of spine
& temples of breath

& steps off
a frieze
to unfreeze
the essence
of life

EVERYTHING IS ALIVE AND HORNY

for Michael McClure, 1932–2020

The limestone imprints
        of Devonian sea creatures
                continue to throb with desire

as do the lichen murals
        on graveyard stones
                and the quarks discharging

their fractional charges
        deep within lichen and stone
                alike

Even Nothing
        is tenderly interpenetrated
                by other, still lovelier Nothings

till out of Chaos
        the Goddess arises
                dripping from the sea of meat

to meet all things
        in sweet embrace
                of their manifold golden bodies

their joy-engendering bodies
        their holy horny miraculous bodies
                perfect in every way

Which is to say—

THERE IS NO FLAW IN THE MASTODON

NO FLAW IN THE ANTELOPE OR MANTIS

NO FLAW IN THE SURGE THAT WAS MICHAEL MCCLURE

WHOSE PERFECT ATOMS NOW DISPERSE

WITH IRREPRESSIBLE ROARING JOY

INTO THE WILD MULTIVERSE

Where energy
          is forever Eternal Delight
                    and his hot mammalian body of work
will never be lost
          to hearing scent or sight

Arrivederci, Corso!

3/26/1930–1/19/2001

Adios, Mad Yak!
& if in the tender scheme of things you do come back,

as a herald bearing scented wine
for those whose criminal nimbi shine,

or a lucid oaken Druid mentoring
lithic hipsters in the art of off-centering,

or a scamming jackal in Pharoah's boat,
or simply as a clear eye in God's mote,

I pray we tarry here to hear you still:
your wide-eyed melodious wiseguy trill,

your deathless heckling of lesser psalmists,
minor croakers & tenured embalmists,

your corvid kvetch & unkempt caw,
of scoffless cosmos the last scofflaw.

Meanwhile, the poems—they're what we keep
as you with Keats & Shelley sleep,

& reading them we have the best
of Gregory, that illumined pest

who drove his picaroon Muse to drink
& climbed Parnassus to pee in the sink.

Deep Listening

for Pauline Oliveros, 1932–2016

the sound
     of snowflakes settling on
     a seismograph   of rose petals
     tossed on the strings of a
     harp   of a single wind chime chinking
     in the memory of an old
     porch   of a cancelled check
     kindled by votive candles   of a
     glyphic typewriter clacking in khufu's
     tomb   of an impecunious
     eurypterid twitching its pincers
     in limestone   of correction fluid
     spilling on a zen scroll   of a pediatrician's
     beeper going off inside a
     coffin   of a plane skywriting 32nd
     notes   of a mezzo emoting an aria in
     american sign language   of some-
     one's mother taking an ax to a
     thrash metal viennese music box   of
     salt rubbed in a ghost's wounds   of grains
     of shadows sifting in the sun's
     hourglass   of a high-tech seraph sampling
     starlight   of your lover moaning on the other
     side of a mirror

III. A Sound a Second for 273 Seconds

A Sound a Second for 273 Seconds

Skein of geese wonka-wonking; cottage settling; creak of stressed pine; babble of nimble creek; ocean oming in hollow shell; cat mewling; crow foraging in compost; antiquarian tapping space bar on antique Remington; cherry bomb detonating in trash can; maestro sneezing at podium; lighter igniting draft card circa 1967; whine of chainsaw heard through rain at twilight; *ouch* following tweezer-pluck of nose hair; cock crowing at sunup; china plate making contact with tiled floor; nude descending staircase; poet hacking up phlegm at lectern; sink filling; sleet peppering parasol; silken, sad, uncertain rustling of each purple curtain; loud *ssshh!* amid library stacks; bottle of bourbon breaking against curb; crunched Dorito; mizzling of housefly; bullet nicking Deer Crossing sign; siren wailing through thick fog; glass object landing in metal recycling bin; flatulence in key of B-flat; swoosh of little brown bat; chittering of black Norwegian rat;

Zildjian cymbal at moment it ceases to shimmer; motorcycle skidding on asphalt; hole being accidentally drilled into Queen Anne walnut cabinet; stridulating cicada; epicurean smacking her lips; persistent hiss emanating from old 78 of Louis Armstrong and His Hot Five; stoner toking roach; hail pelting tin roof; muezzin calling the faithful; clack of Shift key; blues harmonica bending note; canine cracked by pistachio shell; measured breathing of beached whale; apple munched in country graveyard; tweezling mosquito; eight ball plopping into side pocket; snowball spattering jacket of someone's sister; stalactite dripping; drone of Cessna as it apparently bisects Orion's belt; snowflake dissolving in steaming cup of peppermint tea; gleep emitted by malfunctioning urine catheter; pop of plastic packaging bubble; fairy laughter; skritch of ballpoint pen autographing baseball; liquid quibbling of panpipe; hairdryer defrosting drainpipe; crane whooping; long red fingernails raked on blackboard; egg over easy sizzling in skillet; sound of one half-finished haiku, crumpled;

rolodex in full flip; eerie plaint of musical saw; mammoth stamping; sergeant barking command; nun bustling; presses rolling at *Times Picayune*; calico caterwauling; bowl of Kibble nibbled at night by mice; pod bursting; deck of cards being shuffled; hue and cry from several streets away; egret seeking its mate; static between AM stations; Camry being compacted; mustard blurting from plastic container; micturating marmoset; busy signal; flung shoe thwacking U.S. president; groggy sousaphone; vent's dummy burping; peepers chorusing in spring pond; boxing gloves whapping speed bag; popped zit; pager going off in coffin; calving iceberg; distant thunder; skittering chipmunk; tree falling in forest with no one there to hear it; tree falling in forest with someone there to hear it; tree falling on someone in forest;

wind chime chinking at minus-four degrees Fahrenheit; lightning striking satellite dish; baby bawling; sneakers grunching into ice and grit; thrush warbling; turkey gurgling; stork flapping; hog oinking; septuagenarian snoring; rabbi absently drumming fingers on Book of Splendor; crackle of burning haystack; ripping of Velcro bands; echo of cry in canyon; jet flying into skyscraper; freight train grinding through sleet; robotic voice offering menu options; vocalist clearing throat; whistling tea kettle; Etna erupting; mobster firing gun equipped with silencer; wobbling gong; obstreperous klaxon; lemon pennant snapping at used car lot; hand-cranked propeller of candy-striped flying machine; soda fizzing; Doberman growling; mallard quacking; black snake slithering across patio; squeedling shehnai entrancing cobra; pigeon chortling on patinated head of war hero;

clang of hammer on anvil; rap of gavel on bench; whirring of cloud of locusts; bare foot squishing into cow pie; comet making contact with planetary surface; pair of ragged claws, scuttling across the floor of silent sea; wind soughing in stand of conifers; lawn mower in hands of obsessive-compulsive neighbor; ruminant snorting; upended wrestler hitting mat; flat stone skipping across lake; CPR recipient's sharp intake of breath; chattering teeth of polar explorer; scraper scraping paint; angry buzz of wasp entrapped in web; bubbling of hubble-bubble; dromedary expectorating; air escaping deflated balloon; gorilla thumping its chest; mirror shattering; plummeting rivet hitting hard hat; cell phone with particularly obnoxious ringtone going off on forested mountain trail; sticks of kindling suddenly catching; slosh of waterbed underneath couple humping; empty shopping cart sailing across lot into unoccupied Toyota; string of firecrackers welcoming Chinese New Year; Hotpoint Washamatic on spin cycle; cappuccino maker making cappuccino; seagull squealing above landfill; UFO hovering over Woodstock;

orator uncontrollably coughing; wolf howling; coyote yipping; beep-beep-beep of construction vehicle backing up; cash register going ka-*ching*; dragonfly skimming golden cinquefoil; medieval krummhorn being blown for first time in 600 years; *ch-ch-chhhh* of katydid; business-as-usual hum of beehive; clickety-clack of handcar; catcall at Fenway Park; trumpeting swan; slog of galoshes in slush; rifle's retort; calliope playing as carousel turns; bleating of sheep; disquieting snip of moyel's clippers; murmuring starling; pirate's *arrr-rr*; pebble dropped in well; coins clinking in purse; something clonking against outside of bathysphere; floodwater breaching levee; unearthly oscillation of Theremin; fountain plashing; slot machine hitting jackpot; shillelagh whacking British kneecap; kluge plunking into North Atlantic; groan emanating from grating; answering machine answering phone call in abandoned house;

bombinating bumblebee; stuttering nozzle; eddy slapping against pilings; tire iron smashing headlight; dove cooing; empty barrel beaten with the handle of a broom; frailed banjo; musk ox grunting; sleighbell incongruously jingling in late April; out-of-tune viola at American Symphony Orchestra concert; Jaguar honking at Puma that cut it off; accordion dropped from top of Empire State Building; crepitating ice cubes; moose pooping; Bavarian clock recurrently uttering cuckoo; toad croaking; tooted kazoo; G-string snapping on Gibson Les Paul; wheezing of old heap; woodpecker pecking at sycamore; donkey's bray; audience member's audible yawn; another audience member's crimpling of candy wrapper; sandpiper piping; frog squashed by all-weather tire; menu item recited very loudly and slowly to Chinese waiter by American moron; B-52 catching flak; grogger drowning out Haman's name; ceremonial stomp of sumo wrestler; Neanderthal hyoid bone, vibrating;

sonic boom; referee's whistle; new shredding blade in Troy-Bilt Chipper/Vac; sound poet rapidly voicing *leedl-addl-leedl-addl-leedl-addl-leedl-addl*; nail file filing nail; last handful of dirt sprinkled onto casket; tossed garbage can lid resounding in alley; wall of old depot at moment of impact with demolition ball; gibbering ape; something going *blooop* inside an alembic; leopard worrying baboon bone; alligator masticating poodle; mule kicking in stall; bass being bowed; line of coke hoovered by rock star; jumbo trash bag beginning to rip; harp glissando; forearm cluster pummeled on keyboard; vesper pervading French countryside at dusk; tug tugging into foggy harbor; ticking bomb; fax on fritz; construction worker tackling ham sandwich; mare nickering; dial tone; trumpet's tantantara; piggy bank smashed to smithereens; javelin puncturing Etruscan breastplate; vacant shuttle weaving wind; tremendous E major piano chord that ends "A Day in the Life";

muffled oars; whip swishing in Dutch bordello; cow's low on lea; hen's cluck in coop; sobering *ka-blaaam!* of Scud Buster; barbaric yawp; droplet hitting outcrop; King James Bible slammed on table; mallet beginning to tickle marimba; planter cracked by errant shuffleboard disk; street-corner Lothario giving wolf-whistle to busty passerby; bug zapper zapping away on summer night; cricket chirring on dictionary; clanging buoy; cream pie splattering in straight man's face; rusty spring going sproing; black hole droning at 57 octaves below middle C; cowbell announcing whereabouts of cow; glub-glub-glub of swimmer in trouble; landlubber puking over taffrail; horseshoe thudding shy of stake; lion roaring; power mower chewing up pink flamingo; metal sheet beaten during storm scene in *King Lear*; honey bee producing 435 wing vibrations per second in pitch of A; bowling ball scudding into gutter; skyrocket fizzling; Frisbee hitting French door; tied-up ticklee giggling; pulsing heart of patient on operating table;

Scarlatti barfing; Brahms belching; John Cage's long, shaking, silent laughter.

IV. Sonnets, Centos, & Centosonnets

Bible Story

God fashioned Adam from the alphabet,
Eve from the letters R-I-B, which stood for "Rest in Beast."
They shared a pomegranate, fall fell, and the ground got wet.
The land of Nod (known also as Sleep) lay east.

So Eve and Adam took it on the lam
And their little patch of paradise fell to desuetude.
They were now on the outs with I AM THAT I AM
And they were what they were and they rued what they rued.

We rue the same things: the hewing of that Tree
For pulp to make paper for celebrity magazines;
Our loss of innocence (allegedly),
And a time before Death had a home in our genes.

And yet we thank the Serpent for his generosity—
Bestowing on us the beautiful illusion that we're free.

Cemetery Sonnet

Through open gates, find **GATES** forever shut—
No **WALKER** walks, no **FARMER** tills the field;
This **HILL** reclines, this **CARVER** makes no cut;
This **DUNN** is done for good, this **BELL** repealed.

Within this marble valley **WELLS** runs dry,
Ditto **RIVERS**, moistureless as the moon;
This **ROSE** won't bloom, this grounded **BYRD** won't fly;
Both **WOOD** and **WOODS** are permanently hewn.

GOLDEN is pallid now; and ne'er will **GREEN**
Bud forth again in this desolate land;
MOSS harbors lichen, and **BLADES** is not keen;
Naught can be grasped by this bodiless **HAND**.

The caretaker saves what none of them own:
Gray **GRAVES** among graves, gray **STONE** among stone.

Informational Sonnet

Malaysia's capital is Kuala Lumpur.
The largest part of the grass plant is the blade.
Fungi lack chlorophyll, and the Sun, at its core,
is 15 million degrees centigrade.

Farming began about 10,000 B.C.
Tuvalu is only 9.6 square miles.
The act of stinging eviscerates the bee.
Osteoderms are the armor of crocodiles.

The currency of Estonia is the kroon.
Bile is secreted by the liver.
Earth's only natural satellite is the moon.
Bahir is an Arabian word for *river*.

K2 is nearly 9,000 meters high.
Twenty-eight days: the lifespan of a fly.

City Sonnet I

Theban neon throbbing in Ibo streets—
Josephine bringing jungle to the clubs—
Paris, Benares—the city repeats
Its cataract of darting yellow cabs
And airport traffic backed up to the moon.
The towers, high and mighty, start to sway,
Stripping the light fantastic to its ruin,
Stripping it down to payday in Pompeii—
Yet subsequent new towers now arise,
Each of them more hubristic than the rest—
Windows like a mythical giant's eyes,
Watching the tiny landlord thump his chest—
How many foredoomed cities still to come
From fabled ashes of Byzantium?

City Sonnet IV

Through narrow, ancient lanes lost rivers pass—
Indian campgrounds under Union Square;
The city's tale a litany of loss,
Of neighborhoods and woods no longer there;
That church supplanted by a synagogue,
That temple in its turn a Sunni mosque;
The sidewalk here conceals a murky bog
Whose turbid muck preserves a mammoth tusk;
And where today that brothel by the piers,
That hippodrome, that Viennese café?
A building soars—abruptly disappears,
And yet its wraith cannot be wiped away—
Bygone streets pressed into a limestone shelf:
The city is a fossil of itself.

City Sonnet VIII

Here, where Wandering Jew becomes flaneur,
Strolling in neon desert forty years;
Where Philistine becomes a connoisseur
Of New Wave movies; here, where Christ appears
In footlights on the Broadway stage tonight,
Turning the sludge of sewers into wine—
The most outrageous happenstance seems right,
The most haphazard weirdness by design—
Thus we see Miss Liberty in camos,
Or standing in a burka on her perch;
Buddhist monks emerging from stretch limos,
Solar panels gracing an old Dutch church …
Surrealist commonplaces here abide—
Rothkos hang from clotheslines, Lower East Side

The Mind in April

Forsythia a floating yellow cloud
but really an expanse of empty space
much like the sky and forest we behold
in puddles that reflect and fleck our face
and oh the sweetness of this kindled heat
converting ash to ash in Ashley stove
a dancing flame has neither mass nor weight
or so it seems to us, who also love
the flame that gives the eye this marigold
or makes the floral sun to wilt due west
but not until the last day lilies fold
and leave their parting images impressed
upon the mind, where silently they flock
like fossil fish in evanescent rock

One Year's Worth

The ancient wind is playing with its trains
Which streak through sleet, their boxcars full of loss;
Two Colombian French Roast coffee beans
Inhabit (temporarily) a glass
Now drained of bourbon from the night before.
The daylight fading to a violet sigh
As falling snow obliterates the poor,
And wondering if books, like readers, die,
I stroll the churchyard searching for my stone
But find instead, behind archaic clouds,
This broken shard of a ceramic moon,
That nonetheless remains unmarred by words—
As one year's worth of words to no avail
Expands the past's accumulated pile.

Cobbled Sonnet

When, in disgrace with Fortune and men's eyes,
The world will wail thee like a makeless wife;
But 'tis my heart that loves what they despise,
Against confounding age's cruel knife.
So I, made lame by Fortune's dearest spite,
Before the golden tresses of the dead,
And see the brave day sunk in hideous night,
Too base of thee to be rememberéd.
Then can I grieve at grievances foregone
And, like unlettered clerk, still cry 'Amen'
Although I swear it to myself alone
For beauty's pattern to succeeding men.
   Drink up the monarch's plague, this flattery,
   So long as men can breathe or eyes can see.

Canon Fodder VIII

A slumber did my spirit steal
But when I waked, I saw that I saw not;
Care-charmer Sleep, son of the sable Night,
Dark Angel, with thine aching lust
Earth hath not anything to show more fair:
Follow thy fair sun, unhappy shadow.

Give me my scallop-shell of quiet,
Here, in this little Bay,
In a herber green, asleep where I lay,
Jesu, sweete sone dear,
Know then thyself, presume not God to scan;
Let us go hence, my songs; she will not hear.

Marvel of marvels, if I myself shall behold
Not marble, nor the gilded monuments
On the idle hill of summer,
Power above powers, O heavenly Eloquence,
Queen and huntress, chaste and fair,
Rose-cheeked Laura, come;

See the Chariot at hand here of Love,
Take of me what is not my own,
Under the wide and starry sky
Virtue may choose the high or low degree,
We do lie beneath the grass
Your beauty, ripe and calm and fresh

---

from *The New Oxford Book of English Verse,* Index of first lines

Canon Fodder IX

Softly, in the dusk, a woman is singing to me;
Heard melodies are sweet, but those unheard
No one has seen them made or heard them made,
And in short, I was afraid.

Shall I say, I have gone at dusk through narrow streets
To the old Sunday evenings at home, with winter outside
With forest branches and the trodden weed;
Where they have left not one stone on a stone,

One on a side. It comes to little more:
I know the voices dying with a dying fall
Taking me back down the vista of years, till I see
What little town by river or sea-shore,

Is emptied of this folk, this pious morn?
He moves in darkness as it seems to me,
Deferential, glad to be of use,
And pressing the small, poised feet of a mother who smiles
    as she sings.

The initial sequence of the lines is:

D. H. Lawrence, "Piano"
John Keats, "Ode on a Grecian Urn"
Robert Frost, "Mending Wall"
T. S. Eliot, "The Love Song of J. Alfred Prufrock"

"Prufrock," which supplies the last line of the first stanza, supplies the first line of the second stanza, as a line from "Piano" drops down to become the second line, etc. This sequencing holds through the poem.

Centosonnet II

It is not realism makes possible the feast
with its straking smudge and smear;
which, all of a sudden, has ceased—
one makes mistakes in order to appear.

Seen for an instant, a child all in white
under our heavy blankets from Hudson's Bay;
we turn away to the parched plain, the desert light,
and the day still a nymph of a day.

Ah spring, when with a thaw of blue
I tried to fling my shadow at the moon—
it was a dark year for me too,
steaming as usual under a urine-yellow sun.

For more than thirty years we hadn't met.
Life went on as before, and yet—

The poets lending their lines in order of appearance:

Michael Palmer
Amy Clampitt
Charles Simic
Ron Padgett
Sharon Olds
Hayden Carruth
Edwin Denby
Diane Wakoski
Louis Zukofsky
Theodore Roethke
Josephine Miles
May Swenson
Carolyn Kizer
Edward Field

In Which the Poem Suffers the Same Fate as Its Subject

I met a traveler **from** an antique land, who said
Two vast and **trunkless** legs of stone stand
In the desert; near them, on the **sand,**
Half sunk, a **shattered** visage lies, whose frown
And wrinkled lip, **and** sneer of cold command
Tell that its sculptor well those passions read
Which **yet** survive, stamped on these lifeless things,
The hand **that** mocked them and the heart that fed;
And on the pedestal these **words** appear:
"My name is Ozy**man**dias, King of Kings,
Look on my **Works,** ye mighty, and despair!"
Nothing beside remains. Round the **decay**
Of that colossal wreck, boundless and **bare,**
The lone and level **sands** stretch far away.

The Second Coming of the New Colossus

Turning and turning in the widening gyre
The falcon cannot hear the falconer;
Things fall apart; the centre cannot hold;
Mere anarchy is loosed upon

> *A mighty woman, with a torch whose flame*
> *Is the imprisoned lightning, and her name,*
> *Mother of Exiles. From her beacon-hand*

The blood-dimmed tide is loosed, and everywhere
The ceremony of innocence is drowned;
The best lack all conviction, while the worst

> *command*
> *The air-bridged harbor that twin cities frame.*
> *Keep, ancient lands, your storied pomp! cries she*
> *With*

A gaze blank and pitiless as the sun,

> *Send me your tired, your poor,*
> *Your huddled masses*

vexed to nightmare by a rocking cradle,
And what rough beast, its hour come round at last,
Slouches toward Bethlehem to

> *lift my lamp beside the golden door.*

Roman: "The Second Coming," William Butler Yeats
Italics: "The New Colossus," Emma Lazarus

Ten Heretofore Unconnected Things That Are Now Connected

On the road to Damascus, the carcass of a donkey.

○

In the dead letter office, a postcard bearing the likeness of Lauren Bacall addressed to [name illegible], Utopia Parkway, Queens.

○

Just off Route 66 in the Mohave Desert, a colossal "S" fallen from a sign that now reads "HELL."

○

In the Arctic, a slick of petroleum lending rainbow colors to a tundra puddle.

○

Within the Forbidden City, a permitted cricket.

○

On a shelf in Chernobyl, an abandoned matryoshka doll, biding its time inside a slightly bigger abandoned matryoshka doll.

○

Discarded in the Donner Pass, a dispenser of dental floss.

○

On a stage in Stratford-on-Avon, a pierced arras.

○

On the lake isle of Innisfree, a small cabin of clay and wattles made.

○

In a sunsplashed studio in Saugerties, New York, a restless, unsatisfied mind, madly engaged in free association.

The New York Times Book Review: September 17, 2006

I.

Life is better, somehow, if it's a story.

At the outset of the book, George discovers a lesion on his hip.

His poetry, moreover, is terrible.

What he has to guide him is nothing more (or less) than his own voice, which tells him, and his readers, approximately who he is, for the moment.

That said, his insistence on never insisting on anything can become frustrating.

He quotes The Economist: "America is increasingly looking like imperial Britain."

Through all this, we come to understand the shadow his personal history casts over his existence in a London that provides well for the wealthy and white but can prove sterile and dangerous for those who are neither.

But the no-hope atmosphere, the casual brutality, feels affected.

The result is both smutty and pretentious.

Sometimes it seems as if writers of escapist fiction are themselves in need of an escape.

II.

Life is better, somehow, if it's a story.

Well, maybe not in Darfur.

As soon as the fighting began, showbiz kicked in.

Dissections were arranged not just for students, but for paying amphitheater audiences.

But, as with a jaw-droppingly bad movie, just because it's riveting doesn't mean it's pleasurable.

This is not to say that authors of regional crime novels must keep their distance from world events.

They hold tremendous potential energy.

But in their new books, Peter Woit and Lee Smolin say enough is
   enough.
Do you tell would-be writers the crushing truth about their work?
In most cases, they did so—but at a psychological cost.

III.

Life is better, somehow, if it's a story.
Intimidation is only part of the story, however.
"I don't know if I will ever be able to find out who killed him,"
   she writes in the book's opening chapter.
She knows her way around firearms.
She argues, irrefutably, that fringe science has reached ever
   greater heights in military circles.
She's "the bravest, the most adventurous and the most varied"
   actress of her time.
In the early 1960's, she attempted suicide and was sent to a
Jungian psychiatrist, half Australian herself, who would die
   at home in 1970 with a "poisonous" amount of alcohol and
   barbiturates in her body.
Ultimately, Younger must ask the hardest questions faced by any
   shrink: Is it O.K. to kiss one's patient?
She is to be commended for spotlighting the indignities done to
   men and women in the name of science.
It's evident she likes her characters, and you probably will too.

IV.

Life is better, somehow, if it's a story.
But Powers has an unexpected, final story to reveal, "the one I
   don't want to tell, but know I must."
Many of the characters know one another, and just about everyone
   is hiding something: a murder, a child, even a different
   identity.
Even the mayor may be hiding something.

He took kickbacks from old cronies in exchange for permission to
take over Jewish businesses, and by 1943 more than half of the
12,000 administrators of Jewish property in the Paris area had
criminal records.

Meanwhile, there are other rumblings of trouble.

But even the laid-back hippie proprietor of the only inn and
taproom in Paradise senses some freakish disturbance in the
air.

You can see the farce coming, but that's part of the joy of
farce.

True, since the author, now 62, regularly refers to such once-
mythical but now obscure figures as Zsa Zsa Gabor, Yvonne de
Carlo, Elizabeth Berkley and William Faulkner, it is not
certain that the intended reader will understand all the
references.

And damned if any of them do.

V.

Life is better, somehow, if it's a story.

The story opens, embarrassingly, with a paraphrase of Tolstoy:
"There is no mystery to happiness. Unhappy men are all alike."

The melodrama couldn't have been any more overt or less
convincing had it opened, "It was a dark and stormy night."

The course of ejaculation doesn't run much smoother after that.

Restless seeking and venturing I like; cataleptic mugwumpery not
so much.

His obsession clouds his thinking.

It is not clear whether the priest ever became a ballerina.

That's a subject that will require a better book with a bigger
bang.

The unwary reader can be sucked into another world and find it
altogether more fascinating than the one that he or she is
supposed to be living in.

There are also Inuit-like descriptions of snow.

Unreliable Narrator: A Cento

I had taken some steps, useless they had been, and now I went out into the street, agitated, numb. Where would I be when sooner or later, depending on the liveliness of my dissipations, my windfall was used up? I had dinner in a restaurant, then went to a movie. It came to me presently that the moment of creation, where writing was concerned, had little to do with thought. Meanwhile, the truth was, I needed to get laid. I was hardly even embarrassed when I found myself becoming infatuated with a flaming cigarette advertisement on the back-cover of a magazine: a lovely girl, photographed from life, with teasing and sincere brown eyes, posing against the background of a golden tobacco leaf and dressed in a clarion red that seemed a blast of blood-shaking emotion. I was pouring with sweat. Something in her demanded victimization and terror, so she corrupted my dreams, led me into dark places I had no wish to explore. When night came on, I felt that my nude skin was glowing like a light, that the forest would not conceal me. I have not gone deep enough, that's the thing. I walked along arguing with myself about these things, and could not stop; I came on the weightiest objections against the Lord's arbitrariness in letting me suffer for everyone else's sins. I chose a question to which I certainly lacked the answer. I felt like a rat caught in a trap, as though I would have turned and bitten at whatever thing was nearest me. Shall I awake to a consciousness I cannot recognize as mine? If I told you that I am made depressed by a completely still tree but that I am relatively cheered by a tree with a little wind in it whose leaves flutter or whose branches sway, even a little, would you think me strange? I think sometimes that I can tell you very little. Still, despite my lack of faith, I am by nature neither sullen nor wicked. When I was twenty I used to get drunk and then explain that I was a fellow in the style of Descartes. Today I try without success to understand why I stayed away from Paris then, when everything was calling me back. I was unable to fix the boundaries between imagination and memory. I was tired of so much thinking, which is what I did most in those days. In the despairing and solitary state I was in, I considered, as a man aggrieved by a woman will, the NATURE OF WOMEN. That was about the time when I fell in love. I often encountered an anemic young lady on the buses I took to school. The girl was too much, and I couldn't stop looking at her. I felt like bursting into applause. Her face as it was then has been overlaid in my memory by the faces she had later. I see the face of suffering. I see her navy-blue hair pearl-white and cascaded, and scattered with rhinestones. My fingers into her hair like a comb till the hair is tight against the unused nerves between my fingers. To my surprise, she laughed. I knew enough to be honored by this foolery. I stood up with my hands outstretched, turning around so quickly that I almost fell down. By the time I sat down again, I had no choice but to speak. "I'm sorry to have to tell you, but for the moment it just isn't possible for us to go live in another country," I said, sitting down next to her and putting my arm around her. Later, when we were in bed, I felt my heart pounding in my chest, like a great snow owl that has just flew in from Toronto. I had been vaguely hoping for something like the fall of an angel through fourteen abysses, something magnificent and catastrophic, and all there'd been was a little jolt like you get in a bus when it brakes too sharply. Whatever desire or even illusion I may have had to the contrary, perhaps I have not been adequate to what she offered me. I have tried so hard to love others, and I can up to a certain point, and then no further. There was an evening—oh, what a bitter memory, and how I curse it for rising up at this moment—an evening when, propped on my elbows like this, I was leaning out over an invisible garden. I tried not to move; I tried to begin to see in the darkness, but I could not control my breathing and my terror. I saw nothing. I switched on the overhead room light, it was a little flame-shaped bulb in an electrified oil-lamp. I looked around the bedroom, noting its details, remembering them. I looked for incense, that saccharine smell, it had to come from somewhere, but there was no incense burner in the room, nothing in the room but dirty blue overstuffed furniture, a table with a few books scattered over it, and a mirror over the paneling of a Murphy bed. I rolled over on the bed and clenched my fists. I wanted more; more than anything, I wanted to break free. But I knew that the hope was vain. Knowing I was fated never to get out—not in this life, not in this death … I sobbed, or heard someone sobbing I guessed was me, and my face kept hurting. I needed someone to love me so I could figure out reality. Me, an artist, never able to memorize right the lines I wasn't intended to speak or recognizing the cues when I heard them, but somehow trying to take part in the performance, making my exits and entrances blushing, stammering, always backwards and on the wrong side of the stage. That was the first time I peed my pants. I began to leave my body; I began to inhabit the air and the silence. I remember it vividly, but even after all these years I still don't wholly understand my reactions. We have, you and I, only language, at best, if we have anything. I do wish that last sentence had some meaning, since it certainly came close to impressing me for a moment. How much longer can I be amused watching myself watch myself watch myself? Indeed if you are reading carefully it is only you who know me as I am and everyone else, myselves included, is much less certain of this knowledge. How then do I seek a happy life, seeing I have it not, until I can say, where I ought to say it, "It is enough"? My good judgment advises me: Say nothing. I am all the more anxious therefore to arrive at an explanation. I swear, I shall go mad. So it goes with me day by day and age by age, I tell myself. Like Cornelius Agrippa, I am god, I am hero, I am philosopher, I am demon and I am world, which is a tedious way of saying that I do not exist. But surely I recognize a memory image as a memory image, an image of a daydream as the image of a daydream, etc.! I am the descendant of a race whose imaginative and easily excitable temperament has at all times rendered them remarkable; and, in my earliest infancy, I gave evidence of having fully inherited the family character. My father had killed my mother, then killed himself. Yet I was sorry for him. I will not claim innocence for him any more than I would claim it for myself—any more than I could sham surprise, say, at my dreams of murder. "This is the turning point," I thought. Physically speaking it seemed to me I was now becoming rapidly unrecognizable. I also stopped bathing. I dreamed I had entered into the body of a hog, that it was not easy to extricate myself, and that I was wallowing in the most foul mires. "I regret everything," I say aloud to the typewriter. And today I do not raise my eyes from my work. I am an artist, I'm interested in counter- currents, I am a pris- maticist, I work with lenses. Yet truth has always remained for me of an untouched brightness, which is not, as most people believe, the opposite of the colorful world of lies, for they both take their strength—the lies their color, and truth its brightness—out of ha- tred for the real. Recently I have taken more and more to casting up my life, looking for the decisive, the fundamental error that I must surely have made; and I cannot find it. I don't think myself a fool. I have vainly sought a respite in quietude and repose in death, and I can find them nowhere. I have erased, in my books, the borderline between life and death. I clench my fists so as not to be tempted to read the lines of my hand. Then I close my eyes and go to sleep. I now come to the most difficult part of my story. This is what I re- member. I remember a boy, young and delicate, when I first came to New York City. The third time I glanced at him, he was looking at me—smiling. I dragged myself slowly toward him. Though even then, I knew people were capable of damage larger than they were. Naturally I allowed no hint of these reflections to appear to the two plain-clothes policemen. They would shake their jug heads as they listened to how the don seduced me, bamboozled me. I knew I should never have tied up with that guy. What was strange was that all sense of presence, all sense of poetry and style, all sense of idea left me. I should have been prepared for strangeness. I was pushed to utter aloneness, that place where self disappears and merges with space, where everything is hallucinatory and where cause and effect mix. Naturally I'm not going to tell you everything. But I will be the Void, moving without having moved.   Someday I won't be here. A mo- ment before, I too had had an end in view; but now, no plans at all, but I was searching for one again, and I hoped to find something.

For attributions, see page 95.

66

V.   Poems, Prose, and Prose Poems

This Insect of a Mind

as I peed into
the diner's ice-
filled urinal, I
allowed how the shape
of the pissoir's base
reminded me
of the face, or more
precisely the pointed
chin, of the young lady in
a pageboy who, this Sunday
past, sang us a lovely set
of Schubert lieder

A Kabbalist at the Track

He does not dress like a tout. In his shabby
coat, smudgy glasses, pale skin and thin beard, he is
nearly invisible. His rheumy eyes, a pair of ofanim
playing hooky from the seventh heaven, go floating
over the tip sheet. It is the ninth race. Adam Kadmon
has been scratched, most likely by Lilith. The odds
are a googol-to-one that Tardy Moshiach will even
show up for the race, let alone win. But he likes
another longshot, I Tint Her Sex, which he instantly
apprehends as an anagram for Six Thirteen. He places
his bet and picks at a scab—or is it a sapphire?—
on his forehead. Coming down the stretch, the
hooves of his horse, which is a full seven lengths
ahead of Microprosophus, do not make contact with
the turf. He goes to the window, collects his $613,
and goes home. Behind him, the track rolls up like
a scroll, the stubs of tickets are lifted and swirled in
a sudden whirlwind, and the palm trees, their fronds
davening as Shabbos descends on Hollywood Park,
murmur together in a language older than Noah's,
and slowly begin to ignite.

Thirty-six Sentences on Lamed Vovniks

It snows on one of them; rains on another. Both are without shoes. Another is schlepping a heavy box and not complaining; another is stroking the sodden fur of a blind cat. Another of their calling, more recondite still, is employed as a lighthouse keeper at the edge of a lunar sea. We are speaking figuratively, here. That we are speaking at all is a miracle, and the miracle is thanks to them. In their own sight they are small as mesons; to most of us they are smudges on the sills of the world, shmutz on the discarded shmattas of the quotidian. But when one of them has gooseflesh, the universe trembles; when one of them sneezes, there is a momentary brownout throughout the Milky Way. I thought I sussed one out, once, at a soup kitchen in Minneapolis. He was doling out stew to a bunch of losers, not the beautiful kind but the other kind, whose dreams have been flattened by steamrollers of neglect, that bastard offspring of capitalism. But he was beaming, beaming at each of the stubby shadows as they shuffled in front of him, rekindling the dead light in their eyes with the light in his, if only for a moment. If only for a moment the world would stop. If only for a moment that greatest of angels, the one who frees us from suffering but at such cost, would weep for shame. Suppose for a moment that they could know themselves, and not immediately combust, or crumble to dust. How then would it be? Would it mean that Moshiach had finally arrived, redeeming the bleached coupon in each soul? That the mountains would skip like lambs in spring, the sky roll up like a scroll, the seas dissolve like snowflakes? It would mean, of course, there was no longer any need for them, that all of us were now the thirty-six, the pillars of the universe. But that day, by definition, is eternally postponed. "Moshiach" is Hebrew for "mañana," and tomorrow and tomorrow and tomorrow creep in this petty pace from Shabbos to Shabbos, from naked seder to naked seder, to the last syllable of recorded tsuris. And so they linger, continuing to abide in the world, which hides them in plain sight, unassuming as dust. They are gelt not meant to be given; afikomens not meant to be found. Their number remains constant in every age; should one die, another is born in that same instant, somewhere else. Even their mothers do not know who they are. They have manifested on every continent, but always in the villages and cities, always among the throngs. They are not necessarily Jewish, nor even male. They have been cobblers, carpenters, ostlers, masons, blacksmiths, but these days are just as likely to be nurses, garage attendants, pizza flippers, computer technicians. They have not, will never be, brokers, bankers, politicians, attorneys, or journalists. They are flies on the wall that have melded with the wall; they are undetected by any radar, even and especially their own. At this moment, the sun scorches one of them; the wind is making it difficult for another. Neither of them complains. Another is rummaging through a dumpster; still another, sitting on a park bench, is humming as he tosses crumbs to pigeons. They will go on doing these things, being this thing, until the world ends, or finally begins. Did I just hear one of them sneeze? There is no way to know, and for that I say hosanna. Perhaps one of them is even reading this.

Tales of the Hasidic Jazz Masters

I

When Lester Young had finally become Lester Altekacker, he rued having worn a porkpie hat for so many years. After giving it away to a Polish trombonist, he asked his rebbe, "What should I wear in its place, Lady Mordecai?" The sage answered, "Nu? Try a hat made of bacon fat." Said Lester, "But isn't that the same thing, man, the same kind of treyf?" Reb Mordecai replied, "Honey, anyone who can play like you should not have to worry about keeping kosher. You are *not of this world*, my man!"

II

Back when prebop hit the shtetls in the 1840s, Dizzy Gefilte had a steady gig at the Blue Blintz. One night, in the middle of a blistering solo, he took the trumpet out of his mouth and stopped the band. The club owner, as confused as he was angry, said, "Fish—why'd you stop playing?" Replied Dizzy, "To your ears, the music has stopped. But to God's ears, the music continues, and its beauty is undiminished." The club owner mulled this over and finally said, "That's cool. But I'm still taking eighty-percent of the gate."

III

One evening at the 3 Dybbuks, a Talmud scholar who had been sitting at the bar approached Cabala Calloway after the first set. "Man," he said, "the band was so hot on 'Ruby, My Rebbitzen' that I began to tremble. I was shaking all over, and my right hand lost its cunning, and I dropped my Manischewitz. And in that instant," he continued breathlessly, "I saw a pillar of fire ascend from the stage, and seven seraphim wheeling above the bandstand, each of them bearing the sacred letters *yod, hey, vav, hey* in blazing gold." Reb Calloway eyed the young man for a long moment. Then he said, "We didn't play 'Ruby, My Rebbitzen.'"

Meditations on a Melting Snowone

We call them snowmen, but they are sexless. They are snowfolks, or snowones. Like us, they are mostly water. Like us, they have heads, and as a rule the heads have eyes and a nose, sometimes a mouth. The rest of them tends toward lumpy ambiguity, although depending on the skill of their builders, they may have charm, mystery, insouciance, whimsy, even stateliness or nobility. Do they have souls, like scarecrows, or totem poles? Ask the cinders drifting from the chimneys. Or the miner who found the coal for this one's eyes, the farmer who grew the carrot for that one's nose. Ask the sun, into whose bald, draconian abode each snowman goes.

❋

Who squooshed together the first snowman? No one knows. It must have been a child, and it must have been a very long time ago, in a time before time. One imagines a little girl in the Valley of the Caves, in lieu of possessing a doll, patting a confectionary dollop of the Ice Age into a round, firm, somehow comforting image of herself, or her father, a Sno-Magnon. Perhaps the first image of a man or a woman, before color was released from manganese or ochre, was a snowman or a snowwoman, birthed into brief existence by a child.

❋

Like Santa, like the Easter Bunny, the snowman is a secular icon. He doesn't take part in creche assemblages; if he held a menorah, the flames would shorten his life. A snowman, in fact, is an atheist, or at the very least a confirmed agnostic. A pessimist to the end, he harbors no illusions, slipping away into the same elusive element his makers once crawled from, on a hot, Devonian day without snow, 360 million years ago.

❋

Frosty notwithstanding, no snowman has ever achieved immortality. The opposite of an American snowman is an Egyptian mummy. Oh, the mummy melts, too, but condescendingly, at a pace befitting aristocracy. Who would dare, in the presence of Tut, to substitute a carrot for his nose?

❄

Legend has it the great Rabbi Loewe of Prague, before he fashioned a golem out of common clay, built one out of snow. Eight feet high, the snow golem stood behind the synagogue in the frozen ghetto of the medieval city, a mute witness to the splendor of the Word. But despite the arcane letters pressed into its brow, the snow golem's gradual, irreversible liquefaction was the only attribute it shared with the living. Indeed, shortly thereafter, the great Rabbi Loewe melted away, as did all of old Prague, and all of its Jews.

❄

Not all snowfolks are entirely white. A Woodstock woman and her daughter once polka-dotted a snowman with beet juice and carrot juice. The colors froze, and once frozen, didn' t fade; they lasted as long as the chap they adorned, lending color to his cheeks, blood to his veins, rhythm to his shivering, jazz to his attrition in the wind.

❄

Some people make eloquent and magisterial snow sculptures. The scale of these is often grand, their purpose at times devotional; they are to ordinary snowmen what Michelangelo's Moses is to Hummelwerk. My neighbor is one of these geniuses, a Rodin of snow, a Phidias of ice crystals. After the blizzard of '93, he sculpted a monumental St. Francis in his front yard, attended by snowy does, thronged by snowy doves. The work was so extraordinary that at least one local assumed, when she drove by it for the first time, that some company was selling huge St. Francis molds …

※

For every artist who seeks immortality, or what passes for it in this world, there's another artist who prizes evanescence, choosing to work in the most fickle, the most unstable of media. These artists rear castles in the sand, snowmen in the snow. They scorn to document their projects, not taping the unpremeditated, quirky dances they do when alone in their rooms, or the sounds of the sopranino recorders they play on cold nights beneath the constellations. They live when they live and they die when they die, and all that survives them, briefly, is a broken sandal in the sand, a jaunty hat and a corncob pipe in a puddle.

※

Everything dissolves into its own element. A snowman thaws into water. A writer dissolves into words. The words, in turn, dissolve into a page as white as snow. Each word on this page is a nugget of coal, all that's left of a melted writer.

※

I remember seeing, years ago, around Halloween, a cardboard skeleton that someone had placed on the door of Social Services, Food Stamp Division. Likewise, later this season, I can imagine an indigent satirist, building a snowman in front of the same office, and giving it a sign: WILL MELT FOR FOOD

※

A snowman, a scarecrow and a jack o'lantern walk into a bar. I'll have a Tequila Sunrise, the snowman says. I'll have a Grasshopper, says the scarecrow. The jack o'lantern just grins. I'm sorry, guys, the bartender says, but we don't serve cultural atavisms here. The snowman promptly melts on the pool table. Oh, says the bartender to the remaining two, you didn't tell me you had postmodern sensibilities. What can I getcha?

Not every snowman is melted by the sun. Some are melted by the glare of media, the hot griddle of video cameras and the frying pan of the morning papers. These are the snowmen who die, like Christ, of exposure; who deliquesce in the momentary flare, the brief heat, of celebrity. One fine day, they're simultaneously everywhere and nowhere, having melted all over the news.

Snow one is no one.

In Memoriam: Null & Void

for Francesco "Void" Patricolo, 1947–2009

Now literally as well as figuratively,
     but what a time we had when we had it,
          nothing and its better half
performing your favorite odes,
     your specially requested threnodies,
          at divers dives and rumpled clubs
from sea to Chinese sea.
     Terminally inchoate, the critics mizzled,
          too hip for the womb and too ample,
too smart, for the miserly confines
     of skinny bistros. Still, we did find work,
          developing an impressive resumé
of gigs at all-night laundromats,
     subterranean amphitheaters,
          drive-through mortuaries
and undersea hay-bale mazes.
     Guys, you have to be able to work for any audience,
          our manager said,
and so we took it (mostly on the chin)
     to Shriners, Elks, American legionnaires,
          working stiffs and migrant shirkers,
hippies ripped on Acapulco Beige,
     the Hell's Ecologists Motorcycle Club—
          we played for and were castigated
by all of them, and wore that stain
     of failure as a medal of freedom,
          willed obscurity being our raison d'être …
Remember the time we opened for two strippers
     who were twin sisters, Pony and Penny Bright?
          Or the Mensa convention,

at which Void and his anorexic IQ
        decided to do "The Signifying Monkey"?
                A minute and forty seconds in
and forced to cede the stage,
        amid a steady pelting of celery sticks,
                dinner rolls, at least one pair of underwear
and a flaming toupee?
        But man, we *did* bring fire to what we did,
                and the heat of it still warms my heart,
my crotch and the cockles thereof ...
        and sitting here now in the Voidless void,
                testing with a tentative toe
the river we have spent a lifetime crossing,
        whose tenebrous nether bank is thronged
                with erstwhile elderly Republicans,
I must confess it was great to be young with you,
        unsung and uncorrupted,
                two buddies of the mother tongue
without a clue in Kalamazoo,
        lost in the Muck and Meyer
                (another hapless comedy team)
of cultural backwaters,
        up the wazoo of America
                at the end of a terrible century,
busting our humps
        and breaking our hearts
                to make the assholes laugh—
only to see,
        a scant millennium later,
                those same assholes in the mirror,
humbled by Time's damping
        of youthful fire, shorn of ideals
                and stripped of wit

and no longer able
      to "fail, fail again,
            fail better …"

Uut and Uup

"AN ISOTOPE OF CALCIUM IS FIRED AT AMERICIUM,
AND 'SUPERHEAVY' UUT AND UUP ARE BORN."
—*NEW YORK TIMES*, 2/1/04

Talk about your whole life flashing before your eyes, before you have
either a life or eyes! Superheavy survivors of a phantom accident, a
minuscule collision on the rainslick highway of a cyclotron, we de-
cided to take our show on the road, double-billed as elements 113
and 115, Ununtrium & Ununpentium—Uut & Uup for short, or
Nullium & Voidium, as the quarks in the cheap seats called us. In
the tenebrous eternity of 1.2 seconds, we gamely essayed the swift-
est of old soft shoes, as unrehearsed as the birth of the universe—a
shadowy Abbott and ghostly Costello, with no way to know who's
on or who's off first. Even as the boos began and the stage decayed
into dubnium, we were already packed and back in the vasty deep,
two troupers too pooped to pop into the theater of repeatable
phenomena.

Shaving

for Russell Edson

A man confronted the mirror, began to shave his three-day beard.

So this is how it is, the beard muttered. In your absence from the mirror I was finally allowed to bloom, but in your jealousy you would undo what I have nurtured, and in the process destroy me.

I am not destroying you, said the man. I am reaping you. I am merely harvesting the crop of whiskers I planted three days ago, and which has now come to fruition.

Did you say reaping or raping, said the beard.

Oh very well, cried the man, nicking himself on the left of a dimple. You are a failed experiment, a facsimile of a woman's vagina I tried to impress upon my face. But you gave me no pleasure nor even the balm of softness, bristly as you are. Whisker by whisker, it is now my intention to strip you.

Even as you strip me, I mock you to your other face, the beard spat. I mock this parody of jism you squirt from a can, even as I mock the impotence of your ritual.

I am deaf to your scorn, the man said bitterly, whisker by whisker rescinding the beard.

2016 Restrung as a Necklace of Random Moments Encased in Amber

Body creaking and aching, hauled it to the second floor, via the Hillary Step. That evening, moon the color of cloud approaching it, and seen by the creek a young raccoon performing his ablutions. At the concert, delighted to learn that "a-choo!" is "thank you" in Lithuanian. Late snow unyellows forsythia, and late light on upper storeys of brick buildings evokes illuminated manuscripts, with crisscross shadows on fire escapes calling to mind the calligraphy of Irish monks. A soft, subtle wind tousling the oak tops and elder pines—*that* is the angelus makes me bow my head, and voice a prayer that's better left unsaid.

And now it's the green season, infiltrating both sides of the driveway: perfectly cupped suns of marsh marigolds, whitely flowering wild dogwood, red columbines enlivening a rock ledge—just say now to the Tao. A wild turkey shattered Woody's windshield. Grass flattened where seven deer slept. Sitting shivah at JC's, with seven mounted deer heads bearing witness. Shifting shadows of passing trees on back of a big yellow truck—following it for miles was like watching a movie. Meanwhile, starring in her unfilmed feature, Pat is now a spirit catcher, weaving and spinning her arms to gather the invisible, indwelling entities in cars, shrubbery, supermarket parking lots.

Contrarily, we'll live another day, simply to piss it away. Fifty-two bones in the foot, and all of them hurt. At doctor's office, spitting orts of oatmeal on the otherwise antiseptic floor. Sudden city of barely visible springtails, blackening the bluestone, and writhing mealworms in plastic baggie—food for Anita's turtle, Biggie. Expectant spider toting her baby sac. Father Jack: "Celtic eyes are like headlights coming at you from two blocks away." A vast expanse of vigilant phragmites edging the railroad track. Snow premieres on distant peaks: imagination is wilderness.

First night with the gnathic prophylactic, and come morning, first day lily blooms in the studio. Wild geese skimming the surface of Lake Champlain; tough crossing on Essex ferry, masts of small boats clicking like metronomes. Nothing so plaintive as the pre-dawn yowl of an old, deaf, hungry, arthritic cat. Young Poe maiming a mouse in the gladiatorial arena of the bathtub. These withered, bronzing sunflower stalks resemble a host of Giacometti figures, stripped of everything but presence. At dusk a dozen vultures drying their wings, tippy-tops of dead trees ringing the dump. Emerging from dream, this phrase: the "vultures of gratitude." Drone of motors, trilling of cicadas—both belong here.

Mom's hearing aid turns up in a box of chocolates. Gravestone tilting 45 degrees, a granite paddle returning a serve. Tom C: "Sitting is the new smoking." October action for solo performer: lie down in a rural driveway beneath the trees, remain still until completely covered by leaves. Shaken maples, kindling as if they were paper. Old wood burn good. Confusion when she said "tapas bar" which I misheard for "topless bar." The universe doesn't make mistakes—it is one.

Tractors are the poor parade's elephants. Guiding a stubborn chelonian snapper across the road, as turkeys cluck and gurgle in the trees. Mourning in America, as President Narcissus, the Uber Ubu, assumes the throne. Even so, a preternatural violet glow to the forest; the air, the surround, silent as a woodcut of the woods. My 67th voyage around the sun completed, I sit in the studio listening to geese, honking their way south, fleeing what's coming.

Shuffled Months

a sky acutely full of stars
ghosts astream from every surface
spring in her step, the sophomore Persephone passes me on the
  path, re-vitalizing exhausted stalks that once were sunflowers
and I am that moss-capped rock dividing the brook, which ookles
  and blooks around it …
these ants minutely mining a pile of cat puke
these clouds collaged from scraps of handmade paper
this firefly silently interrogating a garden statue …
and sorrow (for now) abandons me, a dozen buzzards abruptly de-
  camping a Dumpster
or mist rising from a mess of perfectly strewn leaves in the pewter
  creek
—o to sight these motley autumnal mountains
through rimed eyeglasses that rhyme with blindness

☆

we are light in its lumpiest form
tresslike creases of light, slowly combed across creekbeds
creatures of luminous autumn, sealed in its amber cartouche
sealed in the shambles the autumn has made of this mountain
now dimly seen the winter sun in coverlet of gauze
white horse and dun horse in orchard, grazing for Godot
above them the Rubenesque cumulus, fatty, crumpled folds of rosy
  cloudflesh
perfect weather for the smoking phantom of a passing freight
perfect day to debate these Episcopal dogwoods, steeped in a pink-
  ness that passeth understanding
poetry an evasive maneuver that always fails, leaving a small bird
  wasted on the windshield
the dead memento of a living flicker of electricity—
a firefly there, not there, in perfect simulation of our lives

✭

"a night unstained by dawn"
and underdusk, the underside of clouds
drove a red Prius to Riverside service
discussing life, death, memory, and rhyme, on company time ...
pinecones crushed by tires in driveway: fossils of extinct marine
    animals, trilopines
and plump woodchuck in day lilies, warily watched by feral cat
all of it splendidly present: the haggard heron in great blue beaver
    pond
the garden spiderwebs domed with dew
a pale pocked moon, floating above red dot of stop light
a dog's ghost making the rocking chair move ...
back in Manhattan I'm whistling Piaf for unimpressed jeunes filles
craving an accordion that fits into a microwave

✭

the year—that is, the Sun—has 12 disciples
one of whom offers a fiery forsythia, lifting forsythical flame-tips
Morgan the calico kneads me as I masturbate,
chasing the rat in this little maze called Reason ...
who can account for this fresh dusting of snow, silversmithing the
    pines
or that smoldering proscenium of ruddy oak and blazing maple,
    overarching a country road
or the way the outside (overgrowth of branches, vines, and profli-
    gate vegetation)
echoes the inside, a chaos of magazines, wrappers, boxes, junk mail
    circulars?
On every bus, the ear as erotic orifice
but not receptive to subway busker strumming to the dead ...
Challenged by truck in front of me: HONK IF YOU DON'T EXIST
I don't, but I do remember Mnemosyne—her sleep interrupted by
    phone calls

things autumn apart
as fall serrates the edges of the air—
"Why don't they make an Alka-Seltzer for grief?"
Might as well go back in time, regather the hunters before the clan
    starts farming ...
It's all a blip, a blink in the eye of eons
a whispered history of white clouds tossed in patchy tableaus on
    crumbling mountains ...
always when crossing water, to remember we slosh as we walk
like the grayskin cat on bluestone wall abutting a mossy gryphon
the gryphon as real as the tiny green tree frog plastered to the
    pane—
adios to them all, to the life that dreams us deeply in the stream
saying goodbye with a steady eye
the afternoon light Vermeering in the trees

Decrepitude encroacheth, but why the unseemly haste?
Zena cornfield now a hayfield,
circling buzzards, eyes on the poets below ...
the house dissolves in lemony light at twilight,
the sky disappears when you get up close to the puddle,
and deer disappearing in wood, as does the year ...
snow, moon, Prednisone,
severe wind wringing confessions from the trees,
the old theater crammed to its creaky capacity,
and featureless and ephemeral as any other shadow
he slipped so peacefully out of this life,
laughing from here to hereafter

nabbed again by the long arm of nostalgia
antique light on brown and leathery leaves

"I remember being immortal, and now I'm not"
watching the clouds out-mountain the mountains
as all the dead convene in heart and head ...
she pockets a rubber band shaped like infinity
unbound hair in a yellow contrail, trailing away behind her
noted by the scrounging crows on much less powerful powerlines ...
sunset a bleeding pink, the sky displaying stigmata
and Time's wing'd chariot doesn't brake for animals
darkly and silently slinking into culverts
condemned to the merely thinkable

✦

the cinema is haunted by the cinema
but *love makes the discovery wisdom abandons*
even here at winter's end when everything looks so shabby
and wandering bees bivouac in bulging eaves
almost theophanic in their apprehensive humming ...
frozen turd in the lower forty
mouse drowning in cat's water bowl
crow strutting with crust of pizza in its beak
and life continues to eat us, while death just clears the table
and lets us know by grace of a swaying tree
wrought by autumn's coppersmith
that the world is its own elegy

✦

feels like I've partially swallowed a toupee
with cop on my tail the whole way over the reservoir ...
dimly remembered even as they occur, the days moving greyly in
    reverie,
the whole fucking engine of Western civ about to blow its tranny
as embers flare in fireplace, Neanderthal TV ...
outside of time I rang the bell so hard the clapper broke,
so hard I hardly heard the cuckoos tweeting at schnitzel eatery,
or sky's pinata popping through the interlacing trees ...

87

floral foam informs a stream that flowers as it flows,
echoing a smokestack plume of otherworldly white;
not a cloud in the sky, not a thought in the head
'cept this: *goodnight, goodnight*

✦

a teardrop of Tabasco
that's our sun in the greater scheme of things
and today it's at sea in the bleachers, glaring at louts and yahoos
and later gilding the spokes of a wheelchair
parked at the end of October by darkening oaks ...
comes a day of bleak and bitter rain
gray as the brain and all its floating ghosts
the erstwhile autumn in post-performance malaise
and these are the days of cloning not cleaning our mess
and sending it to the moon by UPS ...
so, so many friends defiantly frail
the sky at night so clear it almost hurts

✦

The day turned beautiful by mistake
and drenched in ginkgo the eaves dripped yellow
as rusted oaks evoked a dusk by day ...
pleasantly buzzed on wacky weed I fan the light triptastic,
sharing my wonton soup with Homeless Joe,
lugging in logs that night at nine below,
sign reading THINK SPRING in front of nursing home
and someone's bumper: MY OTHER VEHICLE IS THE MA-
    HAYANA ...
thousands of folded unfolding ovine clouds
patches of blue between them alluding to nothing
and nothing doing I pare the cairn of vines
and disentangle the Japanese honeysuckle

✦

firefly passing a match to garden statue
as aspens flicker to wail of a passing train
all of it soundlessly accounted for: the sleeping frogs at pond's
  bottom,
the blown snow making a cake of everyone's mailbox,
the late light foxing the corners of books that can't recall their pre-
  vious lives as trees ...
in a previous life this I was eyeless microbes
void of voice and memory, hence immortal—
where did all that nothing go, this moment of apple bite and chapel
  bell?
lost in a creek that counts each crimp and wrinkle
tossed in a sky that founders in its clouds
misted on the river of sundering numbers
gone like all those elsewhere vees of geese

"love makes the discovery wisdom abandons"—Jack Spicer

Lines Written at My Grave

This fine buffet of sundry dusts and grits
Once answered to the name of Horowitz.
His life, for all its prancing and pretense,
Its failure to employ uncommon sense,
And all its tiny shrines to injured pride
At nearly every neural highwayside,
Was nonetheless a humble one, which sought
To join in bliss the captor and the caught
Who timeshared in his little Yiddish mind
And left linguistic coprolites behind,
Along with tarns of semen spilled into
A dishrag, or a sock, or once, a shoe,
And endless debts, and litigation pending,
And few if any hearts in need of mending.
O traveler, passing swiftly on thy horse,
Believe that this residuum feels remorse
For all the shit it shat beneath the sun
And all the stupider shit it might have done,
Had Time been kind enough to let it stay
In media res this lovely latter day.

Notes on the Poems

A note on Spells

The poems and prose pieces in this volume reflect a long love affair with poetic constraints, originally with traditional English forms but graduating to the playful obsessiveness of the French Oulipo poets. The Spells are acrostics, but whereas most acrostic poems are written north to south, descending vertically from the first letter of the first word on line one to the first letter of the first word on line two, and so on down the page, my acrostics travel west to east, horizontally across the page, so that the seed-word that forms the subject— say, Art—is spelled out in every line. Thus, even if that word is never mentioned in the lines that follow the title, its ghostly presence informs and permeates the poem. But in addition to the spelling out of the poem's subject, this method of composition takes on an incantatory quality, as the constraints particular to this m.o. create obsessively repetitive rhythms that turn the act of writing into the act of casting—or being ensorcelled by—a spell.

A note on "A Sound a Second"

"A Sound a Second for 273 Seconds" was amassed to accompany John Cage's *4'33"*, which comprises four minutes and 33 seconds, or 273 seconds, of ambient, unintentional noises and sounds. These always varying sounds of the surround give the lie to the popular notion that the work is "silent." But "A Sound a Second" subverts the whole point of *4'33"* by impudently imposing a deliberate sound for every second of the piece.

The text is a spin-off from my 10,000 Things, in progress since the early 1990s, which the Guinness Book of Gnomic Utterances has described as the world's longest list poem. As of this writing, 6,900 of the 10,000 things held by the ancient Chinese to constitute the world in all of its variegated richness have been identified and added to the heap. Realistically, I do not expect to complete the list before I say ciao to the Tao.

A note on Centos

The cento—from the Latin for "patchwork"— is a poem or text of any length that consists entirely of foraged borrowings from the work of other poets or writers, ideally resulting in a crazy quilt whose individual patches somehow cohere into a vibrant whole.

My own case for making centos is part and parcel to my abiding concern with environmental issues. To wit: In my house, we recycle organic materials (including cats), metal, glass, paper goods, etc. Some years ago, however, I felt the need to do more, and it dawned on me that it's probably good for both the planet and my overburdened Muse to recycle and adaptively reuse poetry—other people's poetry, that is. Since college, my personal library has harbored vast, bulky, musty anthologies of poetry that haven't been cracked open since the early Pleistocene; unread and neglected, they are sorry reminders of the eventual mortality of so-called "immortal" verse. But consider: as an alternative to burning endless amounts of fuel to stoke the fires of inspiration, poets of every stripe and larcenous persuasion can recover these books and set about sorting and separating similes, mulching metaphors, stripping images, refinishing forgotten sonnets and moldy villanelles, and making them, *voila*, into unprecedented, exciting, and useful new poems.

For example, the poem titled "Cobbled Sonnet" in the Centos section is patched together from the complete sonnets of William Shakespeare (he wrote 154 of them, presumably in those long, gaping lulls between plays). Although some of them are still very much alive in the culture—Sonnet 18, for instance, has become, along with certain verses by Kahlil Gibran, the spoken equivalent of *Pachelbel's Canon* at tedious weddings—many of them languish in obscurity, and would most likely be only too happy to lend their rhymes, allusions, and turns-of-phrase to mash-ups of the "Cobbled Sonnet" kind. In sum, here is a useful way to consider the assembling of centos: if you steal from one poet, it's plagiarism; if you steal from many, it's avant-garde.

Attributions for "Unreliable Narrator"

Where each sentence in "Unreliable Narrator" was taken from, in order of appearance:

1. "The Street (1)," Robert Walser
2. *Confessions of Felix Krull, Confidence Man*, Thomas Mann
3. *Funeral Rites*, Jean Genet
4. *Nexus*, Henry Miller
5. *Burn*, Michael Perkins
6. *Memoirs of Hecate County*, Edmund Wilson
7. *Clea*, Lawrence Durrell
8. *Ice*, Anna Kavan
9. *Beauty's Release*, A. N. Roquelaure (Anne Rice)
10. *A Sport and a Pastime*, James Salter
11. *Hunger*, Knut Hamsun
12. *The Left Hand of Darkness*, Ursula K. Le Guin
13. *Erewhon*, Samuel Butler
14. *Virginie*, John Hawkes
15. *The Interrogative Mood*, Padgett Powell
16. *Haussmann or the Distinction*, Paul LaFarge
17. *Despair*, Vladimir Nabokov
18. *Nausea*, Jean-Paul Sartre
19. *Death Sentence*, Maurice Blanchot
20. *Last Nights of Paris*, Philippe Soupault
21. "The Professor," Lydia Davis
22. *The Marvelous Adventures of Pierre Baptiste*, Patricia Eakins
23. *Cosmi-comics*, Italo Calvino
24. *Confessions of a Mask*, Yukio Mishima
25. *Oracle Night*, Paul Auster
26. *The Debt to Pleasure*, John Lancaster
27. *The Reader*, Bernhard Schlink
28. *Time's Arrow*, Martin Amis
29. *Sheeper*, Irving Rosenthal
30. *Coming Through Slaughter*, Michael Ondaatje
31. *The Gambler*, Fyodor Dostoevsky
32. *The Mask of Apollo*, Mary Renault

33. "The Horla," Guy de Maupassant
34. *The Glorious Ones*, Francine Prose
35. *Aunt Julia and the Scriptwriter*, Mario Vargas Llosa
36. *Sleepers Awake*, Kenneth Patchen
37. *A Night of Serious Drinking*, Rene Daumal
38. *Nadja*, Andre Breton
39. *Under a Glass Bell*, Anais Nin
40. *The Vagabond*, Colette
41. *The Invention of Morel*, Adolfo Bioy Casares
42. *Blue of Noon*, Georges Bataille
43. *The Medusa Frequency*, Russell Hoban
44. *The Archivist*, Martha Cooley
45. *Ask the Dust*, John Fante
46. *Factotum*, Charles Bukowski
47. *Love in Tennessee*, John Bowers
48. *The Last Enchantment*, Mary Stewart
49. *The Stars at Noon*, Denis Johnson
50. *The Book from the Sky*, Robert Kelly
51. *Great Expectations*, Kathy Acker
52. *The Crazy Hunter*, Kay Boyle
53. *Not the End of the World*, Rebecca Stowe
54. *The Lovely Bones*, Alice Sebold
55. *Balzac and the Little Chinese Seamstress*, Dai Sijie
56. *The Derelict Genius of Martin M*, Frank Fagan
57. *Wittgenstein's Mistress*, David Markson
58. *Violence & Defiance*, Herbert Lust
59. "The Sale of What Remains," Ted Castle
60. *The Confessions of Saint Augustine*
61. *The Last Museum*, Brion Gysin
62. *Ecce Homo*, Friedrich Nietzsche
63. *Heart of a Dog*, Mikhail Bulgakov
64. *Grendel*, John Gardner
65. "The Immortal," Jorge Luis Borges
66. *The Brown Book*, Ludwig Wittgenstein
67. "William Wilson," Edgar Allan Poe
68. "The Evening and the Morning and the Night," Octavia Butler

About the Author

Mikhail Horowitz is the author of two collections of collages with texts—*Big League Poets* (City Lights, 1978), and *Ancient Baseball* (Alte Books, 2020). He has published two volumes of poetry, *The Opus of Everything in Nothing Flat* (Red Hill, 1993), and *Rafting Into the Afterlife* (Codhill Press, 2007). His performance work, with jazz and/or acoustic musicians (in particular, Gilles Malkine), has been featured on a dozen CDs, including *The Blues of the Birth* (Sundazed Records), a collection of jazz fables, and the anthology album *Bring It On Home, Vol. II* (Columbia Records). He lives in Saugerties, deep in the woods on the former site of a 19th-century bluestone quarry, with the printmaker Carol Zaloom.